Mary Connell

SLEIGH BELLS & STABLES

ALL AGE READINGS & RESOURCES FOR ADVENT & CHRISTMAS

AMY SCOTT ROBINSON

kevin mayhew

First Published in 2023 by Kevin Mayhew Ltd,

Fengate Farm,

Rattlesden,

Bury St Edmunds,

Suffolk, IP30 0SZ

ISBN (paperback): 9781838581770

ISBN (eBook): 9781838581831

Paperback product code: 1501732

eBook product code: 1501734

CONTENTS

USING THIS BOOK

This book accompanies a children's compilation of Advent and Christmas poems and stories, which is ideal to give as gifts after crib services, donate to a local school or have available as prizes at special events or seasonal assemblies.

The leaders' book contains some additional content, aimed more at adults and whole congregations, to provide further resources for readings at Christmas services and events. It also provides notes and suggestions about how to use the stories in various contexts such as schools and community events.

Content from the children's book appears in this font.

Additional content for the leaders' book appears in this font

Notes and suggestions on how to use or discuss the content appears in this font.

ADVENT

WHAT IS ADVENT?

Advent is the season that leads up to Christmas. It's a time for waiting, hoping and getting ready. Although schools and towns are already decorated with Christmas lights, the insides of churches are darker and quieter during Advent. You can tell that something wonderful is just about to happen.

Advent feels like taking a deep breath, ready to say something important. Like the moment the lights go out before someone brings in a birthday cake. Like being in the cinema before the film begins.

Your Advent calendar probably begins on December 1st, but Advent always starts on a Sunday, four Sundays before Christmas. Sometimes, it begins at the end of November. It is also the start of the church's new year: when Christians go right back to the very beginning of the story.

Christians have all sorts of traditions to help with the Advent waiting. You will find out about some of them in this book.

TINY ADVENT POEMS

These tiny poems, one for every day of Advent, are little pictures to capture the unique Advent atmosphere of anticipation mixed with preparation. The final eight tiny poems follow the O Antiphons (see the next section!)

The Tiny Advent Poems are available in a shareable format for PowerPoint or social media, with beautiful graphics designed by Richard Lyall, at Engage Worship: https://engageworship.org/ideas/tiny-advent-poems

- 1: Advent is the hush in the theatre between the house lights going down and the curtain going up.
- 2: Advent is turning off the lights before you bring in the birthday cake.
- 3: Advent: the conductor raises his baton, the choir takes a collective breath.
- 4: Advent: The night before the wedding, they each read through their old love letters.
- 5: Advent: holiday faces pressed to car windows, who will be the first to see the sea?
- 6: Advent is a new photograph of the family far away - with a travel ticket, all paid.
- 7: Advent: Refugees in a sinking raft spy the lights of the lifeboat.
- 8: Advent: You wake to the smell of coffee and cooked breakfast. Someone is singing in the kitchen.
- 9: Advent: Catch your breath. We're aiming at that mountain in the distance, but isn't the view lovely from this hill?
- 10: Advent: jigsaw bits still scattered, but you've pieced together the frame: ground and sky.
- 11: Advent: Waking in a cold house, hear the heating tick and hum into life. Warmth is on the way.
- 12: Advent is holding the final book in the series for the first time. Creak open the cover. Smell the pages. Read slowly.
- 13: Advent: unseen bulbs asleep in frozen earth. Handwritten markers hold promises of spring colours.
- 14: Advent is a snow cloud behind winter trees, recalling the shape of the leaves.
- 15: Advent: the table is set, the balloons blown up, bunting hung. We jump at each crunch of footsteps on gravel in the driveway.

- **16: Advent: Are we nearly there yet? Yes! Yes, we are!**
- **17: Advent: the house is a mess. Nothing is in its place, some things are missing. I'll never be ready - but help is on the way.**
- **18: Advent: Absently scrolling, you glimpse a forgotten, familiar name. Jump. Gasp. Click...**
- **19: Advent: Amazing story on my family tree. I learn it hungrily, rooting for the root of me.**
- **20: Advent: found a grave old key, cold and weighty. What sacred space did it once unlock? Could it still?**
- **21: Advent: Open the blind. Sunrise: the sky is all the colours. Darkness shrugs away.**
- **22: Advent: Below the balcony, a hush falls. The door opens. Flags wave. Royalty is expected.**
- **23: Advent: a card that says: I can't wait to be with you.**
- **24: Christmas Eve: Text message. Just says: On my way.**

ADVENT IN HISTORY

The word Advent comes from a Latin word which means 'arrival' or 'he is coming'. The church has always seen it as a time for waiting for Jesus. Christians remember the first time Jesus came as a baby, and look forward to a day when he will come back.

In mediaeval churches, monks chanted special songs during Advent. The songs, which were in Latin, called Jesus to come and rescue the world: they called him by lots of different names, such as Emmanuel, Wisdom and Key of David. Sometimes, you will hear a song called *O Come, O Come, Emmanuel* being sung in churches during Advent which still uses some of those ancient words - but in English this time.

People used to fast during Advent: that means that they gave up certain foods, especially fatty and sugary ones, until Christmas. Having to wait to eat those foods helped them to think about how much they were looking forward to Jesus coming!

THE O ANTIPHONS

The section above refers to the O Antiphons, or Great O prayers, used from about the 7th century during the final week of Advent. The images

in them, taken from Old Testament prophecy about the Messiah, can make a wonderfully solid focus for an Advent service, assembly or event. The words of the prayers themselves can be found in Common Worship. The images are as follows:

Date	Latin name	Translation	Suggested object
17th	O Sapientia	Wisdom	A Bible
18th	O Adonai	Lord	An image of Jesus
19th	O Radix Jesse	Root (of Jesse)	A plant
20th	O Clavis David	Key (of David)	A key
21st	O Oriens	Orient/morning star/ dawn	A light, lighthouse, star or picture of sunrise
22nd	O Rex Gentium	King (of all nations)	A crown
23rd	O Emmanuel	God with us	A baby, Jesus figure from crib

These objects can be handled, discussed and prayed with as people consider the questions: what are these items for, what can they do or help with? Who was the Messiah expected to be? How did Jesus fulfil these things? Which of them is most important to me today?

A wonderful thing about the O Antiphons is that the initials of the Latin names, read backwards once you've reached Christmas Eve, spell 'ERO CRAS' which means 'I am coming tomorrow!' I love the idea that the writer of these ancient chants, calling Jesus to come, hid Jesus' reply within the prayers.

ADVENT TRADITIONS

THE ADVENT WREATH

The tradition of the Advent Wreath comes from Germany. The wreath holds four coloured candles in a circle, and a white one in the middle. Every week, starting on a Sunday, one more candle is lit, until the white candle is lit on Christmas day and all five candles are burning.

The coloured candles can be red or purple. Sometimes, the third candle is pink. Each of the coloured candles stands for something. There are various versions, but the one I've always used is that each candle represents a person or group of people who prepared for the coming of Jesus. That way, the candles tell the whole story of God's plan to send Jesus. They are:

Candle 1: God's People, or the Patriarchs: the very first people of God from the Old Testament. This includes the story of Abraham and Sarah.

Candle 2: The Prophets: these were the people who thought and wrote about what it would be like when God's promised saviour would come. They called him 'Messiah', which means 'anointed one'.

Candle 3: John the Baptist: he was Jesus' slightly older cousin, who told everyone that Jesus was the saviour they were waiting for.

Candle 4: Mary: she was the mother of Jesus, who was told by an angel that she would have God's son and that he would save the world.

Candle 5: Jesus, the light of the world.

THE ADVENT WREATH SONG

Here is a song to sing as you light your Advent wreath. Every week, you add an extra verse and chorus to go with the candle you are lighting. It goes to the tune of 'Angels From The Realms Of Glory'.

Advent candle, shining brightly,
tell us how the story starts!
Tell how Abraham and Sarah
followed God with faithful hearts!

We are waiting,
waiting for our saviour,
We are waiting,
waiting for our saviour king!

Advent candles, shining brightly,
Tell us of the prophets brave,
those who spoke about Messiah,
said the Lord would come and save!

We are waiting…

Advent candles, shining brightly,
Tell of John the Baptist's call,
He prepared the way for Jesus,
Naming him the Lord of all

We are waiting…

Advent candles, shining brightly,
Sing the song of Mary's praise,
Of the God who keeps his promise
Now until the end of days

We are waiting…

Advent candles, shining brightly,
Tell us what the angels say:
Peace on earth, to God the glory,
Jesus Christ is born today!

Alleluia,
Now we have our saviour,
Alleluia,
Now we have our saviour king!

This song is easy to use in church as you light the Advent wreath before the service, because it goes to the tune of a well-known carol, so the organist should have the music! Unless you have copies available for the congregation, it can be easier to teach the chorus and have a soloist sing the week's verse. You can either add an extra verse and chorus every week, or if that takes too long, simply sing a chorus, the week's verse and then the chorus again, perhaps saving the whole thing for the lighting of the final Christmas candle.

SANTONS DE NOËL

In France, many families have a display of little figures called santons. They begin with an ordinary crib scene: Mary, Joseph, baby Jesus, shepherds and kings. But there are hundreds more of the figures, and some collections look like a little town: there are people doing every kind of trade, children and elderly people, and all sorts of animals too. Every year, a few more are bought and added to the collection. It's a way of remembering that the wonderful news of the first Christmas spreads out into everyday life and affects everybody, even today.

It's not possible to buy Santons in England, but in my family, we use Playmobil to do the same thing. Every year we add a few more to our collection, and every day of Advent we place a few more figures into the growing scene. We've been collecting for so many years that we now have a snow scene, a Christmas market, a Santa's workshop, a church with a carol service and a nativity play going on, a family at home - and, of course, the stable with the nativity characters. During Advent, though, we don't put Mary, Joseph or Jesus in the stable. Where are they? Read about the next tradition to find out!

POSADAS

In Mexico, people celebrate posadas during the last week of Advent. A posada is a way of telling the story of Mary and Joseph's journey to Bethlehem before Jesus was born, and their search for somewhere to stay. People dress up as Mary and Joseph and go house to house, or sometimes just act out the journey in one place. They sing a song with a question and answer, with Mary and Joseph singing the questions and the people in the houses - the innkeepers - singing the answers. When Mary and Joseph are finally allowed in, there is a party.

Some churches and schools follow the idea of posadas by sending toy versions of Mary and Joseph around to a different house every night of Advent. In our house, we use the figures of Mary, Joseph and the donkey from our Playmobil santons collection and move them around the house. Every morning, they have reached a new place, and the children have to find them! They visit every room of the house during Advent, and finish their journey when they reach the stable on Christmas Eve.

Posadas are a great community activity for Advent. The Mary and Joseph figures often travel around with a 'diary' or scrapbook for their hosts to add photographs and notes about what they have done or seen during their visit. Hosts keep them for a day and then pass them on to a friend or neighbour. The difficulty is tracking the figures down at the end of Advent so that they are ready for next year.

JESSE TREE

A Jesse tree is an old way of telling the story from the beginning of the Bible up until the birth of Jesus. Some very old churches still have Jesse trees in their stained glass windows or painted on the walls: they were not an Advent tradition then, but they were used to teach people about the family of Jesus in the days before many people had their own Bibles, or even knew how to read.

A Jesse tree can be any kind of tree; some people use a little Christmas tree, or a bunch of twigs in a vase. Every day of Advent, they read a story, make a decoration to remind them of the story and hang it on the tree. By Christmas day, the tree is full of decorations.

You can find many lists of suggested stories and Bible verses by searching for Jesse trees online.

Here is a list of Jesse Tree stories with suggestions of images for the decorations. In this list, every story apart from the first one is based on one character or pair of characters, so depending on time you could tell more than one story for the character, or find a creative way to explore their lives. You could also use my book, *Tales from the Jesse Tree*, although the story list is slightly different.

The Bible references given here are not intended as readings for church: some are very long! They are for you to see which part of the story could be covered, and decide how best to retell or use it. For some, for example Moses, you could add more to the suggested story or take a smaller portion. Many of the stories are available in children's Bibles, but the Jesse tree isn't just for children: a Bible study group, for example, might like to read all the passages privately before discussing them.

	Character	Reference	Decoration
1	Creation	Genesis 1,2:1-3	A globe
2	Adam and Eve	Genesis 3	A tree, snake or apple
3	Noah	Genesis 6:9-9:17	A rainbow or boat
4	Abraham	Genesis 12:1-9	A tent
5	Sarah	Genesis 18:1-15	Trees, a loaf of bread
6	Isaac	Genesis 21:1-7,22:1-18	A ram, a bundle of wood
7	Rebekah	Genesis 24	A veil, camel, water jar or well
8	Jacob and Esau	Genesis 27,28:10-16	A ladder, angels
9	Leah and Rachel	Genesis 29:16-30	Two women
10	Joseph	Genesis 37,39-46:7	A coloured coat
11	Miriam and Jochabed	Exodus 1 and 2	A basket, rushes, a river
12	Moses	Exodus 3 and 7-12:41	A burning bush
13	Joshua	Joshua 1	A book, tablet of law
14	Rahab	Joshua 2 and 6:1-25	A scarlet ribbon, or a trumpet
15	Ruth	Ruth (whole book)	A sheaf of wheat
16	Samuel and Jesse	1 Samuel 16:1-13	Anointing oil, or a sheep
17	David	1 Samuel 17	A sling with stones
18	Elijah	1 Kings 18	A raincloud
19	Jonah	Jonah (whole book)	A big fish
20	Daniel	Daniel 1,3,5 and 6:1-24	A lion, fire
21	Isaiah	Isaiah 9:27, 11:1-10	A light, a tree
22	Micah	Micah 5:1-5, 7:18-20	The town of Bethlehem
23	Elizabeth and Zechariah	Luke 1:1-23, 57-80	A writing tablet (with 'His name is John' written on it)
24	Mary and Joseph	Luke 1:26-38, Matthew 1:18-24	An angel

ADVENT CALENDARS

There are so many different kinds of Advent calendars! Paper ones have little doors to open, with pictures behind them; some have chocolates. Some have boxes, bags or pouches with daily treats. Some have stickers to add to a scene, or charms to add to a bracelet, or part of a story to read every day. Some are online or available as apps, with a little game to play or video to watch every day. How many different kinds of Advent calendar can you spot in the shops?

You can make your own Advent calendar by sticking 24 doors to a piece of paper with tape, and drawing pictures behind them. Or you could try a craft calendar by cutting up old Christmas cards and choosing a picture every day to glue to a piece of paper and make a collage. Or you could add a bead to a string every day and finish with a bracelet. There are so many ways to count the days! Which is your favourite?

ADVENT CANDLES

An Advent candle has the numbers 1 to 24 written down the length of it. Every day, you light the candle and let it burn past the number of that day - but don't forget to blow it out before it reaches the next day's number! When I was little, my family used to light our Advent candle with the words 'The light of Christ is coming to the world'.

You can make an Advent candle out of any ordinary candle by carving the numbers into the wax with the point of a biro or a cocktail stick - be careful and get a grown-up to help if it's sharp.

COMMUNITY ADVENT

A church or a school has a great opportunity to involve the local community in an Advent activity. Here are some ideas:

ADVENT WINDOWS

You will need to be able to find 24 people in the local community who have windows facing out onto the street and are willing to join in. This might be in an area like a village or housing estate, or along a route such as the road to school or church. Give each of them a large sheet of card with a number (1-24) on one side of it. Their challenge is to decorate the other side with a festive scene, then put it in their window with the number facing outwards, remembering to turn it around and reveal the picture on the date of their number!

When we tried this, there was a wonderful variety of pictures, from single people with an artistic flair to whole families with a love of glitter and tissue paper.

In other years we handed out shapes instead of paper: cardboard stars, for example. This worked as well if not better for recognition, but perhaps gave less opportunity for individuality.

This can also be run like a treasure hunt by adding a letter to the corner of each card on the picture side. The letters all spell a message, and by Christmas day anyone who can tell you the message wins a prize. (Lines from carols work well. NOW PROCLAIM MESSIAH'S BIRTH has exactly 24 letters!)

ADVENT STONES

This one takes more preparation, but less ongoing effort to run. Begin with a number of painted stones, which could be decorated by children at an Advent event or in school. They need to be weatherproof, so acrylic paint pens and varnish are a good idea. The stones could be painted with festive pictures, or with each of the nativity scene characters, and they then need a unique hashtag painted on the back, so that anyone picking them up can look on social media to find the instructions.

The stones are then sent out into the community at the beginning of Advent to be hidden in plain sight around the local area. (Don't hide them underneath and behind things - the idea is that they're easy to spot, eg at the doorway of the shop, on the steps of the slide at the playground, etc.)

People who find the stones should photograph them and hide them again in a different place, leaving a clue on social media along with the hashtag, so that everyone who is playing can search for clues and hunt for the stones.

When we tried this, we put an additional message on the stones that they would be exchanged for chocolate if brought to the Christmas Eve service. But don't expect to see them all come back. Some will have left the area, some will have been taken home and some are just too well hidden!

ADVENT EVENT

Holding an event may not have such a wide community reach as the other ideas, and involves more cost and organisation, but it is a great way to invite the community to participate in Advent. Hold it just before Advent begins, at the end of November. The idea is to equip people to follow Advent in their own homes, so as well as space for a short, welcoming explanatory talk, offer craft stations where people can make calendars, crib figures and wreaths (depending on your budget, these could be at any level; from birthday cake candles pushed into playdoh to playing with holly, ivy and oasis!) Baker Ross and Hobbycraft have seasonal kits to make this easier, especially if you are expecting lots of children, but the crafts can be tailored to the community you are inviting. You may wish to print out some handouts about how each craft can then be used during the season, with prayers for lighting each candle, for example. Festive refreshments and plenty of space and time to chat make the event an annual hit.

ADVENT STORIES

PET PREPARATIONS

Harry put Ziggy, the school hamster, gently back into her cage and clicked the door shut. He looked up at his mum. 'See, mum? I did it! I looked after her all weekend! I fed her and changed her water, and I even scooped her poopy bedding out this morning.' Harry looked longingly at the fluffy, sand-coloured hamster racing around in her little wheel. 'Please can I have a pet of my own now? Please, mum, please?'

Mum smiled and picked up the cage to carry it to the car. 'Wait until Christmas and you'll see,' she said.

Harry could hardly believe his ears. Did that mean yes? At last! A hamster of his very own! He only had to wait - he checked the calendar - another three weeks. He might burst before then! And if he did well taking care of a little pet, then maybe - one day - he might be allowed something bigger. Maybe even - he hardly dared hope - a dog!

As soon as he got home from school that day, Harry raced up to his room. Ziggy's cage had sat on his desk, but he needed that space for colouring and homework, so his new hamster would have to have a more permanent home. Harry began to tidy the space on top of his chest of drawers, finding new homes for all his dragon figurines and scooping his Lego builds into the top drawer with his socks. There! That would be the perfect place for a cage.

Mum came in to call him for dinner. 'It looks nice and tidy in here,' she said.

'I've cleared a space for my new hamster's cage!' explained Harry.

'I see,' smiled Mum, 'but wait until Christmas, Harry.'

Harry couldn't wait that long. There were things to do! On the walk home from school the following Monday, he ran ahead and gazed through the window of the pet shop. 'Mum, can I use my pocket money to buy a water bottle for my new hamster? Or a little bed, or a wheel?'

'Wait until Christmas, Harry,' said Mum.

The following week, Mum investigated a strange smell in Harry's room and found a shoebox full of mouldy apple slices and grapes.

'Ziggy likes them, so I've been saving them from snack time for my new hamster,' explained Harry.

'Please wait until Christmas, Harry,' said Mum, as she threw them in the bin.

School finished for the holiday, and Harry brought home a plastic bag full of things they'd been making: a secret Christmas card for Mum, decorations for the tree, a paper chain and a drawing of a hamster with a Santa hat on. He stuck the drawing on the wall above his empty chest of drawers. 'Mum, when are we getting the cage for my new hamster?' he asked.

'Wait until Christmas, Harry!' said Mum.

'I'm *trying* to wait, but I'm worried I won't be ready,' said Harry. 'What if I get my hamster and it doesn't have anything it needs?'

'Just a few more days, Harry. You'll have to trust me,' said Mum.

At last, Christmas day came. Harry and Mum went to church and sang carols. When they came home, Grandpa and Grandma were there to share Christmas lunch. Harry could hardly sit still long enough to eat his turkey and Christmas pudding. It was nearly time!

After lunch, they all went through to the sitting room and looked at the bright parcels under the tree. Harry looked for something the shape of a cage. He put his ear to a big square package, but he couldn't hear any scuffling noises. Perhaps the hamster was asleep?

'Can I open one now?' he asked.

'Hang on, Harry' said Mum, 'Grandpa's just popped out. Wait for him to come back.'

More waiting! Harry jumped up and down on the spot, watching the door.

Then Grandpa came in. He had something in his hand: it looked like the end of a rope. The rope trailed down to the floor. And on the other end of the rope was a fluffy, wiggly, sandy-coloured and incredibly cute...puppy!

Harry dropped to his knees. Grandpa let go of the lead, and the puppy raced across the floor, wagging its tail, and leapt into Harry's lap.

'Happy Christmas, Harry,' smiled Mum. 'We thought it was time you had a pet of your own.'

'I never guessed it would be a PUPPY!' gasped Harry. 'I thought you were just getting me a hamster!'

'I know!' laughed Mum. 'Imagine if I'd let you buy a cage and a wheel! It's hard to get ready for something if you don't know what you're getting ready for, isn't it? I hope you're not disappointed that it's not a hamster.'

'Of course not!' grinned Harry, ruffling his excited puppy's fur. 'This is the best Christmas present ever!'

Advent is all about waiting and getting ready for God's promises to come true when he sends Jesus. Here are some stories and poems about people who were waiting for Jesus - even though, at the time, they didn't know exactly who they were waiting for or how long it would take. Some of them lived hundreds of years before Jesus, but they all knew that God's promises would come true one day, and trusted that it would be worth waiting for.

As you can see from its conclusion, this story is a great way to begin talking to children about waiting and preparing, and to introduce the concept of Advent. If you use it in a school assembly, you could ask the question: if Harry had known he was getting a puppy, what would he have done differently to prepare? After discussion, you could go on to explain that Advent is all about getting ready for Christmas, but it's hard to prepare when you don't know exactly what you're preparing for.

This gives an opening to talk about what Christians believe about Christmas, or about what people were waiting for before Jesus came and what Christians are waiting for today. You can explain at the children's level that Christians believe Jesus will come again one day to make the world perfect again, and that Advent is about remembering the first time as well as looking forward to the second time. Invite ideas about what it would look like to be ready for Jesus.

ABRAHAM AND GOD'S PROMISES

This story is adapted from the version in my book, Tales From The Jesse Tree. It comes from the Bible and can be found in the book of Genesis, beginning in chapter 12.

God called Abram and his wife Sarai out of their home to travel to a new land. 'I will make a great nation from you, and bless it, and I will make your name great,' God promised.

Abram and Sarai travelled for a long time and had all sorts of adventures and troubles. When Abram started to lose heart, God said, 'Don't be afraid, Abram, I will make a great nation from you'.

Abram said, 'That's all very well, Lord, but I don't see your promises coming true. Sarai and I haven't had any children, so where will this great nation come from?'

God said, 'Look down at the sand. Can you count the grains of sand?'

Abram said, 'Of course not. There are far too many to count.'

God said, 'You will have children, and your children will have children, and your children's children will have children until there are more people in your family than there are grains of sand.'

And they kept travelling, on and on wherever God led them. More adventures. More troubles. When Abram started to lose heart, God said, 'Don't be afraid, Abram, I will make a great nation from you'.

Abram said, 'That's all very well, Lord, but I don't see your promises coming true. Sarai and I haven't had any children, so where will this great nation come from?'

But God said, 'Look up at the stars. Can you count the stars?'

Abram said, 'Of course not. There are far too many to count.'

God said, 'You will have children, and your children will have children, and your children's children will have children until there are more people in your family than there are stars in the sky.'

And they kept travelling.

It took a long time. It took a very long time. But God kept making the same promise. He even changed Abram's name to Abraham, which means 'Father of many people', and Sarai's name to Sarah, which means 'Princess'.

Then at last, at long, long last, when they were both very old, Abraham and Sarah had a son. They called him Isaac, which means laughter, because the very idea that she could still have a baby made old Sarah laugh out loud. They were so happy.

But one day when Isaac was a little boy, God said, 'Abraham, take Isaac up that mountain, and kill him as a sacrifice to me.'

So Abraham told Isaac that they were going on a journey to worship God, and off they went up the mountain together. Isaac noticed that their donkey was carrying some wood. 'It's to make a fire for a sacrifice,' said Abraham.

'But we don't have anything to sacrifice on the fire,' said Isaac.

'God will provide something when we get there,' replied Abraham.

At the top of the mountain, Abraham tied Isaac up. He put him on top of the wood. He took out a knife. He raised it above his head...he took a deep breath...

'ABRAHAM! STOP!'

Abraham froze, the knife in mid-air.

'Don't hurt your son, Abraham!' said God. 'You have trusted in my promises so much that you would even have given me your son. You have shown me that you know I will never break my promises! I promise that Isaac will grow up and have children, and his children will have children, and his children's children will have children until there are more people in your family than grains of sand and more than the stars in the sky. And they will all be blessed because of your faith in me.'

COVENANT

You made a covenant of coloured light
    with Noah, that you would not end the earth
    but work a better way to set it right,
    return it to its perfect, sinless birth.
    Rain and light, light and rain:
    bring your kingdom here again.

You made a covenant with Abraham
    that he would hear a newborn child's first cry
    repeated in a billion grains of sand
    uplifted to the deepest starry sky.
    Sand and stars, stars and sand:
    heaven and earth at your command.

You made a covenant with Israel
    that you would write your law on human hearts,
    and every guilty wrong, since first we fell,
    would find forgiveness in your love at last.
    Law and grace, grace and law:
    bind us to you evermore.

And you have made a covenant with me
    that through your son, who died and rose again
    I shall not perish everlastingly
    but come at last to see the Peace-Prince reign.
    Death and life, life and death:
    Save me at my final breath.

UNCLE MICAH

This is a story about the prophet Micah, who has his own book in the Bible. You can find some of the things he said hidden away in this story.

'Please, Uncle Micah! Please take me to the city with you!' I tugged playfully on my uncle's belt, while my sister Anna, who was much shorter, hung on to the edge of his robe. Uncle Micah took a few steps across the floor to pick up his bag, and Anna slid along behind him, giggling. He turned around and looked at us both seriously.

'Why would you want to come to the city? It's a terrible place. I'm only going there to tell them how terrible a place it is, and then I shall come back here to my nice quiet farm.' He bent down to place a solemn finger on Anna's nose. 'I shall only be a few days, little niece.'

'It can't be that terrible,' I objected, 'since Mama and Papa go there all the time to take our vegetables to market. They come back with lovely things for us - sweets and clothes and my tambourine. I want to see the places that sell all those things!'

'Oh, let them go with you, Micah,' said my mother, appearing in the doorway. 'They'll only be under my feet here, with all the seeds to plant. I'm sure you'll keep them safe.'

'It's a very long walk,' said Uncle Micah, 'and only one of you can ride my poor old donkey at once.'

'I don't mind walking,' I said, and Anna piped up: 'I'll run!'

'Oh, very well!' my uncle sighed, 'Fetch your coats and bags. Perhaps it's time that you learned what Jerusalem is really like.' He smiled at us both, though his eyes looked sad.

It was a long journey into the city. We even slept in a field on the way, and then spent the early morning walking in from the city gate through lots of little streets. We were both sleepy, but the colours, sounds and smells kept Anna sitting up straight on Uncle's donkey. People bustled past us carrying bundles to market, pushing and shoving their way through. Once, a very rich man on a fine horse approached, and his servants held us back against a wall until he had gone past.

'That wasn't fair,' complained Anna. 'Why should he go ahead of us?'

'That's right, Anna. What do I always tell you two that God wants us to do?' asked Uncle Micah.

'To do justly, love mercy and walk humbly with God,' we chorused.

'Exactly. Well, the city people don't behave that way,' said Uncle Micah. He scratched his chin through his bristly beard. 'Keep looking out for things that aren't fair, Anna, and you'll make a fine prophet.'

Once we reached the market, I found it hard to stay by Uncle Micah's side. There was a stall full of musical instruments - little tambourines like mine, but also harps and lyres, trumpets and drums! I itched to give them a try, but when I reached out as we went past, the woman behind the stall swatted my hand away with her stick. 'No touching without paying!' she barked. I put my hands behind my back as we walked past other stalls so that I wouldn't be tempted by the soft fabrics, the fresh warm cakes that smelled so good, the boxes of cute fluffy ducklings or the shiny necklaces and bangles.

We stopped by a stall to watch grain being measured out for customers. As the stallholder poured the grain into the scale, he leaned the bag on it so that it looked heavier. I pulled on Uncle Micah's sleeve. 'Did you see that? He cheated! The customer paid full price for less grain! Mama and Papa would never do that!'

Uncle Micah nodded. 'This is what I'm here for,' he whispered. Then he pulled himself up to his full height, took a deep breath, and began to speak in a louder shout than Anna and I had ever heard him use.

'Listen up, you wicked lot! Hear what God is saying to the city! He sees your trick scales and deceitful weights. The rich men of the city are all violent, they cheat and tell lies and make the poor suffer. Jerusalem will be destroyed if you carry on like this!'

Not many people stopped to listen. A few people laughed or jeered. The cheating grain seller shouted, 'Get this old man away from my stall! He's bad for business!' Then some people from the stalls nearby threw rotten vegetables at us. Anna started to cry. Uncle Micah said a few more things, then led us away.

We stayed at an inn that evening. When the innkeeper saw us, she frowned. 'Double the price for a child,' she said.

'But why, when they're half the size?' asked Uncle Micah.

'They're messier and louder,' she scowled.

In our room, Anna asked, 'Why was that woman so mean?'

'City people only ever think about how much money they can make,' said Uncle Micah. 'They're doing it because it's how the richest people behave. They steal from the poor and think they can have whatever they like.'

'I'm glad you come here to tell them off,' said Anna.

'I want to do more than tell them off!' I said, wiping some slimy vegetable seeds from my tunic. 'I can't believe the grain seller gets away with cheating like that. I want to stop him somehow.'

'That's why you will make a fine prophet one day,' said Uncle Micah. He was doing his sad-eyed smile again. 'Evil people will do what they do. We must only do justly, love mercy and walk humbly with our God.'

The next day, we travelled home. It was good to be out of the city, but I was still feeling angry about everything we'd seen.

'If nobody will listen to you, Uncle, what's the point of telling them?' I asked. 'There's nothing we can do about them, is there? Especially not me and Anna. You keep saying we'll make good prophets, but I don't want to be a prophet like you and never be listened to. Anyway, we're too small.'

Uncle Micah put his hand on my shoulder. His other arm was supporting Anna, half asleep on the back of the donkey.

'Listen,' he said, and his voice was as gentle as the sun rising over our farm in the distance. 'There's something else I tell them. Even though we have evil leaders and we fight wars now, one day a new leader will come. He will come from the little town of Bethlehem, so small that nobody thinks of it as a great place. He will live with the poor like us, and he will lead like a shepherd looking after his sheep, not like a king stealing from his people. Then there will be peace. You see, God always forgives. God is full of love. And God keeps his promises.'

'But when will all that happen, Uncle?' I asked.

'Sometimes, when a seed has been planted, we just have to wait,' said my uncle. 'And in the meantime, we must...?'

'Do justly, love mercy and walk humbly with our God?'

'Exactly,' said Uncle Micah.

The references hidden in this story are from Micah 6:8, Micah 5:2-5, and Micah 7:18-20. Micah came from a country life to prophesy in Jerusalem, taking particular issue with the injustices of the rich and powerful against the poor and helpless (Micah 2:1-2) and, among many other things, mentioning dishonest scales and false weights (Micah 6:10-12). The rest is imagination.

ISAIAH

You see the rich things hidden in the plain.
You see a sapling rooted in dry earth
and know it speaks of sacrifice and pain;
you see divinity, a death, a birth.

You see a green shoot growing from dead wood,
your mind is cast back onto ancient kings:
then forward centuries through wars and blood
until you gaze with hope at holy things:

a sign enough to tame the red-toothed wild.
An ox and lion are stabled, eating straw,
and wolves led out to pasture by a child
whose hand, unharmed, shuts off the viper's door.

The circle solved, the reign of peace restored
in all my holy mountain, says the Lord.

This sonnet refers to Isaiah 11:1-9.

JOHN THE WRECKING BALL

John the Baptist was Jesus' cousin. He was talking about Jesus just before Jesus started his own teaching and people began to follow him. Different bits of John's story can be found in the Bible near the beginning of the books of Matthew, Mark, Luke and John.

John the Baptist,
John Bulldozer,
John the wrecking ball:
levelling mountains, laying roads,
shouting out his call:
'No time left!
The Saviour comes!
Get ready, one and all!'

Prepare the way,
Make straight the path,
and fill the valleys in;
knock down the mountains of your doubts,
make smooth the soil of sin,
the Lord is coming, shout it out!
His glory will be seen!

John the Baptist,
wild and hairy,
eats what he can find.
Not one to tiptoe round the truth,
He says what's on his mind:
No time left!
The Kingdom comes!
Now don't get left behind!

. . .

Prepare the way,
make straight the path,
for we are grass and flowers;
we die and fall, but our Lord lives
and now He comes in power.
Fear not, Judah,
shout good news:
His word will live forever!

John the Baptist
calls the people:
'Hear the words I say,
turn from sin and be baptised,
wash your wrongs away!
No time left!
that longed-for Lord
is here today, today!'

The Bible verses referred to in this poem include Isaiah 40:3-11 and Mark 1:1-8. It works well performed by several voices, with one person reading the John the Baptist sections, and a chorus of people reading the italicised 'Prepare the way' sections.

MARY AND ELIZABETH

This story can be found in the first chapter of Luke. The baby that Elizabeth is having is John the Baptist, Jesus' cousin.

Two women are running to meet each other.

One of them is running up the hill, and the other one is running down the hill.

They are waving, and laughing, and holding open their arms as they run towards each other.

The one running down the hill is running rather slowly, partly because it's not easy to run downhill without tripping; partly because she is quite an old woman; and mostly because she is pregnant. You can see the bump where she has a baby inside.

The one running up the hill is running quite fast. She is much younger, and she can't wait to get there. In fact, she is also pregnant, but you can't tell yet. Her baby is much, much smaller and newer, still tucked away secretly inside.

The one running downhill is called Elizabeth, and the one running uphill is called Mary. When they meet, they throw their arms around each other, and as they hug, Elizabeth's baby gives a big leap and a kick from inside her. Both women feel it and start laughing: laughing because it's so wonderful. Laughing because it all seems so impossible. Laughing because it's true.

'Mary! It's so good to see you!' says Elizabeth. 'Look, even my baby knows about the miracle that has happened to you. You're going to have a baby too, and he will be my Lord, and your Lord. But how did you know to come here?'

'I saw an angel!' Mary says breathlessly. 'A messenger from God! He told me all about my baby, but he also told me that you are having a baby too - after all these years!'

'It should be impossible,' says Elizabeth. 'Zechariah and I are so old. But nothing is impossible with God.'

'That's exactly what the angel said to me!' says Mary. 'My baby is impossible, too. Joseph and I aren't married yet, and we've never even been alone together. The angel said that my baby is the son of God: God's own promise come true.'

'Two impossible babies!' says Elizabeth, and the two of them start laughing: laughing because it's so wonderful. Laughing because it all seems so impossible. Laughing because it's true.

'Do you know, I think Zechariah saw an angel, too,' says Elizabeth. 'But I can't be sure, because he was in the temple when it happened - and when he came out, he couldn't speak. But he looked amazed.'

'Joseph saw an angel as well!' says Mary. 'The same one that I did, but later. The angel told him that I really was having God's son and that everything would be all right.'

'So that's three angelic visits and two confused husbands,' says Elizabeth.

'And two special babies, and two happy women,' says Mary.

'And one amazing God,' says Elizabeth, and then they are both laughing again. Laughing because it's so wonderful. Laughing because it all seems so impossible. Laughing because it's true.

MARY'S SONG

When Mary met her cousin Elizabeth, she sang a song of praise which is sometimes called the Magnificat. You can look it up in a Bible: it's in Luke 1, verses 46-55. Here is a shorter version of Mary's song: you can read the word 'Magnificat' down the left-hand side. Why not try writing your own version?

My soul magnifies the Lord,
And my spirit rejoices in my saviour!
Generations will call me blessed,
Naming God as holy and mighty.
In strength, he has scattered the proud,
Fed the hungry and left the rich empty.
Israel will see his mercy again.
Children of Israel, you know what he promised
Abraham and his family forever?
Those things are happening now.

IF GOD CAME DOWN FROM HEAVEN

The people who prepared for Jesus had lots of ideas about what he would be like. What do you think

If God came down from heaven,
What would he look like?
Would he dress in funky clothing
And ride a motorbike?
Or would he be all old and wise
And have a long white beard?
Perhaps he'd look like Santa Claus.
Perhaps he'd just look weird.

If God came down from heaven,
I wonder what he'd do?
Would he go round zapping people,
Or parting seas in two?
Would he act like a magician,
Pull a rabbit from his hat?
Or like the genie in Aladdin,
Granting wishes just like that?

If God came down from heaven,
I wonder what he'd say?
Would he be sad or angry,
Or would he think the world's OK?
If I invited him to my house,
Would he act like a mate,
Or would he be a grumpy grown-up
And think my room's a state?

God did come down from heaven,
But he was hard to see.
First, he looked like a baby,
Then, just a kid, like me.
He said all sorts of brilliant things.
He said they were all true.
He said he came because he loved us,
And he said I should tell you.

CHRISTMAS

CHRISTMAS TRADITIONS

CHRISTMAS TREE

Why do we bring trees into our houses at Christmas time? They look pretty, and the real ones smell good, but it's a bit strange, isn't it?!

Christmas trees started with mediaeval 'mystery plays', which were put on to show the stories of the Bible to ordinary people who, in those days, couldn't read. The story of the Garden of Eden was shown at Christmas time, when there were no leaves on the trees: so instead people used trees that are still green in the winter, like firs and pines. They hung fruits on the trees to be the fruit that Adam and Eve took, and they placed a snake in the tree to be the serpent who tempted Eve to take the fruit. The fruits turned into the baubles we have on our trees today, and the snake became the long garlands that we hang around the tree, like tinsel or paperchains.

The plays were performed all over Europe, although they went in and out of fashion, and sometimes the trees were decorated even if there was no play. The tradition stayed in some countries, like Germany, and died out in others. Gradually, people forgot the original reason for the trees.

Queen Victoria was the one who brought the tradition to England from Germany, and was shown in a photograph with her Christmas tree, which made everybody want one - and so they became popular again.

Although they come from a tradition that was over 600 years old, we've been putting trees in our houses for less than 200 years.

Here is a story about the very first Christmas tree.

THE PARADISE TREE

Agnes sat by the fire, embroidering an apron. It was to be a Christmas present for her mother, so she hoped she would be able to finish it by Twelfth Night. Agnes' mother was a seamstress and her father was a tailor, so Agnes had been learning to sew ever since she could hold a needle. All the same, it was tricky to make the little fir tree in the forest scene she was stitching look the same on both sides. Agnes sighed, and unpicked a branch that looked a little longer than the others. As she did so, the door creaked open and her father came in, a flurry of snow behind him.

'Great news, Agnes!' he said, as he took off his hood and stamped snow from his boots. 'In this year's mystery plays, the Tailors' Guild has been given the Paradise Play!'

Agnes put her sewing down and clapped her hands. She loved the mystery plays, which brightened up the winter days with stories from the Bible, all acted by the townspeople. Each play was put on by a different group of people who worked in the same trade, called a guild.

'Which one is the Paradise Play?' she asked.

'Don't you remember from last year? It's the story of Adam and Eve in Paradise, and how they ate the apple. It's the one that plays on Christmas Eve, before the Nativity shows how Christ came to put it right,' said her father. 'We shall have a wagon for our stage, set up in the town square with a fruit tree on it, and I shall play the evil ssserpent!' He hissed as he reached out to draw Agnes into a tight hug, and she giggled.

'Can I be Eve, and you'll persuade me to eat the fruit?'

'Eve has rather a lot of lines to learn. And it's the tailors who should have the big parts. Perhaps we'll let you be an animal in Eden, though. A squirrel? Or a bunny?'

'I can't wait!' said Agnes.

Rehearsals began, and soon Agnes' father was muttering his lines to himself in a snakey voice as he went about his work. Agnes, her mother and her sisters, meanwhile, were sewing the costumes: fig leaves for

Adam and Eve, all sorts of furs and feathers for the animals, and a fine white gown embroidered with flames for the angel who guards the gate of Paradise. The apron for Agnes' mother sank to the bottom of her workbasket as they stitched late into the evening every day, burning through tallow candles until it was too dark to see their needles. The mystery plays were a good chance for the guilds to show off their skills and encourage everyone to buy their wares, so everything had to be perfect.

The day before the performance, they put the wagon together. The families of the other tailors had stitched flowers, creatures and magical fruits for the garden of Paradise. They had even made a long snake puppet, glistening with scales made of oyster shells that caught the light of the candles. But something was missing.

'Who was supposed to make the tree?' asked Agnes' father. The tailors, seamstresses and embroiderers all looked at each other and shrugged. Not one of them could sew an entire tree.

'Last year, it was the carpenters' guild who had this play, and they carved their tree,' said Agnes' mother. Everybody shrugged again. Nobody in the tailors' guild could carve.

'Can we use a real little tree?' suggested Agnes.

'We might have to, but it's the middle of winter,' said her father. 'It will look very bare.'

'Perhaps I can sew some leaves and stitch them to the branches?' said Agnes.

'You can try,' said her father, 'but there's only one night left, and it's already dark.'

Back at home, Agnes picked up her workbasket and rummaged through it, looking for scraps of green fabric. She pulled out the forgotten apron, with its little fir tree, and smiled.

The next day, Christmas Eve, the townspeople gathered for the performance. The wagon stage was all lit up with candles: the flowers gleamed with bright colours, and Agnes and the other children in their animal costumes made a perfect picture of Paradise. There in the middle stood a little fir tree, its branches green despite the winter, hung with all sorts of fantastical fruits, and with a shining snake wound around it from the top to the bottom, its scales sparkling in the candlelight. The crowd gasped at the crafters' skill as the snake moved, opened its mouth and seemed to speak; and the play began.

This story is a good chance to explain why the Paradise Play was put on just before Christmas: the problem caused by Adam and Eve was solved by Jesus, who makes peace between earth and heaven so that God can one day restore the earth to how it was in Eden. Christmas was a time to tell the whole story of the Gospel. In that way, our Christmas trees can be another reminder of the reason we celebrate.

DECORATIONS

How do you decorate your house at Christmas time? Do you have decorations in every room of the house, or just one? Are they the same every year? Do you have any favourites? Perhaps you make some of them. In our family we enjoy cutting snowflakes out of paper, making paper bag stars and sticking paper chains together, as well as looking forward to seeing familiar baubles coming out of their box.

People used to decorate their houses with evergreen plants like holly, ivy and fir, especially if they had bright red berries. Other decorations existed as well, though, especially in richer households. Did you know that tinsel was first invented in 1610 in Germany, and was made from real silver?

Traditionally, decorations go up on Christmas Eve and don't come down again for twelve days, which is the whole season of Christmas. These days, many people like to put them up sooner, during Advent.

Here is a story about a girl who had an unusual helper to decorate her house one Christmas.

MARY, SCARY AND THE CHRISTMAS TREE FAIRY

Once upon a very close to Christmas time, in a tiny one-room cottage by the forest, a girl called Mary climbed shivering out of the bed she shared with her mother - and screamed.

In the corner by the door and right up on the ceiling, was a scary, hairy, very much bigger than ordinary...spider!

'Get it out! Get it out!' screamed Mary, but Mary's mother shook her head. 'It's so cold outside,' she said, 'and we don't have enough money to help anybody else this Christmas. At least we can give a warm home to a spider. It won't hurt us.'

That day, Mary and her mother began to get ready for Christmas. Mary's mum counted her pennies and frowned. Enough maybe for one present for Mary...a few treats for Christmas dinner...a bit of fuel for the fire. Nothing else.

Mary went to find the box of decorations in the shed, although she had to walk past the spider - shudder! There was a wooden crib set with nativity figures, a candlestick for the window, and Mary's very favourite

- the Christmas tree fairy. Mary lifted her out of the box and unwrapped her pretty face and her shiny wings and wand.

'Mother, when are we getting our Christmas tree?' she asked.

'There's no extra money for a tree this year, Mary,' said her mother.

'But the fairy has to sit on top of something!' insisted Mary.

So Mary walked past the spider (shudder!) to the door, and went out to the forest to look for something to use as a Christmas tree. After a while, she found a fallen pine branch that was small enough for her to drag it through the snow. She brought it back to the cottage, found a pot, and stuck it in.

It was just a branch, stuck in a pot, and leaning over. Mary brought it inside anyway, past the spider (shudder!) and placed it by the window. Then she picked up the fairy and placed her on the top.

Now it was just a branch, stuck in a pot, leaning over, with a fairy on top. It looked a bit silly. 'It's better than nothing,' said Mary. 'At least we have a tree on Christmas Eve.'

That night, while Mary and her mum slept in their bed, the Christmas tree fairy shook her wings, stretched, yawned and looked around the cold little room. No fire? No presents? No feast waiting? This wasn't like the Christmases she remembered. Then she caught sight of the spider: 'Aaah!'

'What's the matter?' asked the spider, grumpily. 'Mary has been shuddering at me all day. Do I really look that scary?'

'Well,' said the fairy, 'you are hairy, and much bigger than ordinary, but I can see now that you're not really scary. Would you mind coming over here and giving me a hand? You see, this tree is just a branch, stuck in a pot and leaning over, with a fairy on top. It could do with some more decorations.'

The spider scuttled over across the ceiling and dropped down on a long, silver thread. Then he went round and round the tree branch, spinning his webs between the pine needles. He climbed back to the ceiling to admire his work.

'Well, now it's just a branch, stuck in a pot, leaning over, with a fairy on top, covered in cobwebs,' he said. 'I tried to help, but cobwebs are the only thing I know how to do.'

'Don't worry,' said the fairy, and she waved her silver wand.

When Mary woke up on Christmas morning, she didn't scream or shudder - she gasped! Her Christmas tree was still a branch, stuck in a pot, leaning over with the fairy on top - but now it was wrapped in shiny silver tinsel, and every corner of the room where a cobweb had been now shone with silver too. The fairy on top of the tree was still and silent, and gave no clues; but beside the door, a spider swung on a glittering silver thread.

When telling this story to children, I have actions that go with the refrain: 'It was just a branch, stuck in a pot (bend knees) leaning over (lean over) with a fairy on top (arms flapping like wings). I don't teach it, but by the last time round, the children are often joining in.

This is a good one to introduce a talk about how God can use and transform what we have to offer, even if we don't feel it's very much.

NATIVITY PLAYS

A nativity is a play that tells the story of the first Christmas. Have you ever been in one? What part would you like to act, if you could? There's Mary and Joseph, of course, and then there are shepherds, angels and kings. Sometimes there's a grumpy innkeeper or two, and there are lots of animals. Nativity plays don't always tell the story exactly the way it goes in the Bible, but they're lots of fun and help us to think about the reason we're celebrating.

Here is a story about the person who first invented the nativity play.

ST FRANCIS AND THE CHRISTMAS SHEEP

Once long ago, a little lamb lived in a field with his mother and a flock of other sheep.

One day, at the end of spring, as the weather was getting warmer and the lambs were starting to eat the fresh grass instead of their mothers' milk, the lamb's owner picked him up and carried him away from the field. The terrified lamb bleated as his owner tied his legs together, strapped him to a pole and walked towards the market.

Before they had gone very far, a man in a brown robe and cloak stopped them and asked, 'Where are you taking that little lamb, brother? He looks too small to be away from his mother.'

'That may be, monk, but I need the money. My daughter is ill. This one is the biggest of the flock, and will have to be sold for slaughter so that I can buy medicine.'

Dangling upside down, the lamb started to shake with fear.

'I have no money, brother, but take my cloak in exchange for your lamb: it's a good one, and will be more valuable than the lamb if you sell it,' said the monk.

The lamb's owner agreed, handed over the lamb, and hurried away with the cloak. The monk knelt beside the lamb and gently untied him. 'Come, little brother,' he said, 'you shall not be harmed. I will name you…what will I name you?'

'Maaah!' bleated the lamb.

'Martinello, then!' laughed the monk.

Martinello and his new friend soon arrived at a big building, where many other men in the same brown robes greeted them at the door. They all laughed when they saw Martinello. 'What's Francis rescued this time? This is not a monastery, it's a zoo!' said one of them.

Francis - that was the monk's name - winked at Martinello and said, 'Now, little brother, if you are to stay here you must be a good monk. Praise God quietly, and don't bother the brothers!'

Martinello came along to church every Sunday, although he didn't understand it - it was all in Latin. But Francis looked so moved by the words that the sheep was moved too, and bowed his knees and bleated along to the music. The brothers soon got used to his being there.

The weather got colder and Martinello grew a thick fleece. He loved Francis and enjoyed being in the monastery, but he often thought of his mother, brothers and sisters out in the chilly fields.

One day, Martinello found Francis looking sad. He crept up to his side and bleated. Francis put a hand on his woolly head. 'It will soon be Christmas, the joyful time when we remember our Lord Jesus Christ being born as a baby to save mankind. All the townspeople will be coming to the Mass to celebrate, but they won't understand it, because it's in Latin and all the carols are in Latin too. Jesus was born for the poor and needy, but the poor and needy never get to hear and understand it!'

Francis scratched Martinello between the ears. 'I think I might need your help, little brother.'

Over the next few weeks, Martinello learnt some Christmas carols along with the brothers, bleating tunefully as they sang in Latin: 'Saeculorum saeculis!'

'Very good, Martinello,' smiled Francis. 'That means 'Evermore and evermore,' you know. I have a plan: will you do what I tell you?'

So on Christmas Eve at midnight, when the time came for the Christmas mass, Francis led the brothers out of the monastery and out of the town. There in a cave, they found a wax baby lying on a bed of straw, with a man and woman dressed up as Mary and Joseph kneeling beside him. There was a donkey and an ox, and there, kneeling in the straw next to the baby was Martinello, bleating for all he was worth: 'Evermore and evermore!'

Francis said the whole mass in the cave. 'This is how it really happened! Christ was born for the poor and needy, surrounded by animals,' he said. 'Angels sang to shepherds in the fields and told them to find the baby. Look, here they come with their sheep!'

Sure enough, shepherds and sheep crowded around the opening of the cave. And there among them was Martinello's mother! Martinello ran to her, bleating joyfully.

At the end of the mass, Francis went to find Martinello and discovered him with his family. There, too, was the shepherd who had sold him. Francis smiled at them.

'Brother, how is your daughter?'

'She is well, brother Francis,' said the shepherd. A little girl came out from behind him. She stroked Martinello's head.

Francis nodded. 'Brother, little sister, I will give you back your sheep: he is with his family again. You don't have to pay me back for the cloak. But promise me that you will never harm Martinello or any of his family, because they are creatures of God who were blessed on this holy night'. The shepherd solemnly promised, thanked Francis, and led his flock back to the field, with Martinello bouncing happily along by his mother's side, still singing: 'Evermore and evermore!'

We now know Francis as Saint Francis. He invented the nativity play that night. There are lots of stories about Francis' love for animals, which is why he is the patron saint of animals. As for Martinello, if you listen carefully to a field of sheep, especially at Christmas time, you can still sometimes hear his descendants singing: 'Evermore and evermore!'

The 'evermore and evermore' refrain in this story is taken from the Christmas carol, Of The Father's Heart Begotten, which itself comes from a mediaeval Latin plainchant. The Latin words were written in the 4th century, so they could well have been chanted by Francis! This story could be linked with that carol in a carol service. It is also suited to crib services, which some say also stem from Francis's innovation.

CRIB SERVICES

A crib service is a little bit like a nativity play, but rather than having people dressed up as the characters, some churches have a model called a crib scene. It's a stable or cave shape, with models of each of the people and animals from the Christmas story. The models are placed in the crib one by one while the story is read from the Bible, and carols are sung. Afterwards, everyone stands around the crib to see the scene and sing carols, and sometimes small gifts are given out. Crib services often take place in churches on Christmas Eve, so that the scene is ready for Christmas Day. Sometimes, the figure of baby Jesus is not placed into the crib scene until midnight or Christmas morning.

Here is a poem that would be fun to read while you look at a crib scene. Can you find all the different characters?

THIS IS THE BOX

This is the box, with hay for an ox, that became a bed for Jesus.

These are the creatures, curious and silly, that fed from the box with hay for an ox, that became a bed for Jesus.

• • •

This is the stable, dark and chilly, that was home to the creatures curious and silly, that fed from the box with hay for an ox, that became a bed for Jesus.

This is the couple, weary and worn, that stayed in the stable dark and chilly, that was home to the creatures curious and silly, that fed from the box with hay for an ox, that became a bed for Jesus.

This is the baby newly born, who came to the couple all weary and worn, that stayed in the stable dark and chilly, that was home to the creatures curious and silly, that fed from the box with hay for an ox, that became a bed for Jesus.

These are the shepherds who left their flocks to look for the baby newly born, who came to the couple all weary and worn, that stayed in the stable dark and chilly, that was home to the creatures curious and silly, that fed from the box with hay for an ox, that became a bed for Jesus.

These are the angels with curly locks, who sang to the shepherds, who left their flocks to look for the baby newly born, who came to the couple all weary and worn, that stayed in the stable dark and chilly, that was home to the creatures curious and silly, that fed from the box with hay for an ox, that became a bed for Jesus.

This is the star all gleaming bright, which shone on the angels with curly locks, who sang to the shepherds, who left their flocks to look for the baby newly born, who came to the couple all weary and worn, that stayed in the stable dark and chilly, that was home to the creatures curious and silly, that fed from the box with hay for an ox, that became a bed for Jesus.

. . .

These are the wise men in the night, who followed the star all gleaming bright, which shone on the angels with curly locks, who sang to the shepherds, who left their flocks to look for the baby newly born, who came to the couple all weary and worn, that stayed in the stable dark and chilly, that was home to the creatures curious and silly, that fed from the box with hay for an ox, that became a bed for Jesus.

And here are we all, some big, some small, to feel the peace, to see the glory, to hear once more the Christmas story...

To hear of the wise men in the night, who followed the star all gleaming bright, which shone on the angels with curly locks, who sang to the shepherds, who left their flocks to look for the baby newly born, who came to the couple all weary and worn, that stayed in the stable dark and chilly, that was home to the creatures curious and silly, that fed from the box with hay for an ox, that became a bed for Jesus.

This story, based on the nursery rhyme 'The house that Jack built', is fun to do with actions. You could try:

- *Box: holding arms in a square shape*
- *Creatures: hands like horns on your head, and a silly face*
- *Stable: hands above head in a roof shape*
- *Couple all weary and worn: back of the hand to forehead in a melodramatic 'weary' look*
- *Baby: arms rocking an invisible baby*
- *Shepherds: hand shielding eyes to 'look for the baby'*
- *Angels: both hands make 'curly locks' in a spiral down from your head on both sides of the face*
- *Star: a hand opening and shutting in a flashing motion, or with fingers twinkling*
- *Wise men: hands holding an invisible telescope up to eye*

It does take a bit of rehearsal to get them going fast enough and in the right order!

WHAT DO WE KNOW?

There is always a balancing act, at Christmas, between retelling the story in the way that we've traditionally received it - the nativity play story - and pointing out that the Biblical version is both simpler and much more complicated, more amazing and more terrifying than the comfortable version we know. For some people, discovering that the Bible doesn't actually mention a stable, an innkeeper and three kings is a point of historical curiosity. For others, it can be like having the rug pulled from under their feet. This is a poem about that.

What is there in the Bible when you read about Christ's birth?

There isn't any stable, though we know there was a manger.
There isn't any donkey, though we know there was a journey.
There aren't innkeepers, though we know the house was full.

There might have been three magi - we only know they brought three gifts.
They could have all been kings - we only know they found a king.
They could have come on camels, but the camels aren't recorded.

We can be fairly sure it wasn't snowing.

We know there was a baby, and he was God among us.
We know that there were angels, shepherds, danger, joy, confusion.
We know that there was worship and we know that there were warnings,
and we know that there was weeping.

. . .

We know he wasn't born to safety, luxury or riches,
but born to us - and for us - and as vulnerable as we are.

What is there in the Bible when you read about Christ's birth?
There's Jesus - at last, Jesus - and the hope of peace on earth.

STOCKINGS AND SANTA

What do you hang up on Christmas Eve? Not everyone uses a stocking. I know someone who puts out a pillowcase, hoping for lots of presents! In some countries in Europe, children put their shoes or slippers by the fireplace, or by the door or window.

And who are you waiting for? Some people call him Father Christmas, and some say Santa Claus. Different countries have different names for the person who brings them presents, too; and in some places, that person comes on a different day. Sometimes it's the three kings who bring gifts on January 6th; and in Syria, it's a little camel.

In many countries, St Nicholas brings the gifts, and often on his own day, which is December 6th. But perhaps he's not so different from the one who fills our stockings: 'Santa' means 'Saint', and 'Claus' is short for 'Nicholas' in German. Saint Nicholas is the patron saint of children. He is a bishop, so he wears red clothes and a pointy red hat, and has a long white beard. There are lots of stories told about his generosity. I wonder what it would be like to meet him?

WHEN MAX MET SANTA

'Twas the night before Christmas, and snug in his room,
little Max was awake with a feeling of gloom.
He thought of his sister, the evening before,
how she'd shouted, and thrown all her food on the floor,
and the terrible words that were yelled by their mum:
'If you are so naughty, then SANTA WON'T COME!'

Max thought of his sister, ignoring the warning,
and thought of her sad empty stocking next morning,
and thought of her face when she saw nothing there,
and thought until thinking was too much to bear.

With visions of tragedy stuck in his head,
Max broke a rule. He got out of his bed.
Then he crept round his room, like a true Christmas elf,
taking small toys from each cupboard and shelf
and placing them into his book bag from school
counting enough to make one stocking full.

Then quickly downstairs he went, quiet as a cat,
and into the sitting room - but, who was that?
In the hat and the beard and the coat white and red,
who turned round and spoke: 'Max, you should be in bed!'

'Santa, it's you!' Max said, 'Please don't get mad!
I was worried because my poor sister was bad,
I thought that she might have been crossed off your list,
And so I brought presents, in case hers got missed.'

Santa Claus nodded and said, 'Max, don't go -

I'll tell you a secret that you ought to know.
When I was your age, Max, I heard someone say
That Jesus, whose birthday is on Christmas Day,
was given by God to us all, every one,
no matter what terrible things we had done.
He grew up to teach us, and died in the end,
To come back to life as our saviour and friend.
And so, when I learned of God's great gift to me,
I knew I should give just as generously.
My gifts are like God's: his forgiveness, I learned,
Is never deserved and can never be earned.
I once gave my coat to a thief who was cold,
And to three desperate sisters, I gave bags of gold.
I don't have a list of the good and the bad,
I simply pass on the free gift that I've had.'

Then Santa Claus brought out some gifts from his sack,
and merrily handed them over to Max:
'All these for your sister - you'd nothing to fear!
Now, how about lending a hand while you're here?'
So while Santa filled one stocking, Max filled one too,
And he said, 'When I grow up, I hope I'm like you.'
Santa smiled broadly, and said with a wink,
'Yes, you'd make an excellent Santa, I think.'
And Max heard him call, as he watched him depart,
'There's forgiveness for all - and for all, a new start!'

This poem touches lightly on some of the legends about St Nicholas, without suggesting that Santa himself doesn't exist, of course. I hope that it goes some way towards countering some of the more harmful parts of the modern Santa story - the idea of having to be good enough to receive - and replaces them with the grace and love of the true Christmas story. It has been a popular one to read at Carol and Crib services, or secular events when a lighter touch is needed.

MIDNIGHT MASS

In some churches, midnight mass, or midnight communion, is a special service held late at night on Christmas Eve. It isn't always at midnight, but it often finishes around midnight. It is the first church service of Christmas. People take communion to remember the moment of Jesus' birth, and that he came to be with us.

The first time I was allowed to join my parents and go to church at midnight was very special and exciting. Here is a poem about how it felt.

EVEN THOUGH I HAVEN'T BEEN TO BED

It's midnight, but the church is full of people,
all smiling as the final words are said.
It's midnight, but now Christmas day has started -
even though I haven't been to bed.

We walk outside. The night is cold and starry,
the moon's a bauble on a silver thread.
We've listened, prayed and sung, and now it's Christmas -
even though I haven't been to bed.

In church, we went and knelt down by the altar,
the grown-ups each had wine and broken bread;
and I was blessed and kept, and now it's Christmas,
even though I haven't been to bed.

Although we haven't opened any presents,
or spotted Santa's reindeer and his sled,
I know that Christmas day has really started,
even though I haven't been to bed.

We creep indoors, and on the hallway table,

I find the Christmas figures in their shed.
I place the baby Jesus in the centre.
It's Christmas day - and now it's time for bed.

CHRISTMAS DINNER

Wherever Christmas is celebrated, there are traditional Christmas foods. In the UK we have turkey, mince pies and Christmas pudding, but in other countries, they have all sorts of different foods - for example, in Denmark, they eat pickled herring, in Ethiopia there's a spicy chicken stew with hard-boiled eggs, and in Poland, there's a special meal with twelve dishes - one for each day of Christmas - which include beetroot soup, fish and dumplings.

The special dinner isn't eaten at the same time everywhere. In England, we tend to have the meal on Christmas day, either at lunchtime, dinnertime or somewhere in between. But in many European countries, it's eaten after sundown on Christmas Eve, when the Advent fast is finally over. Some Orthodox countries don't celebrate Christmas at all until January, or have another, bigger celebration then.

What's your favourite Christmas food? Perhaps your family has its own traditions, and without them, it just wouldn't taste like Christmas.

THE ICE MARKET MIRACLE

English Christmases used to be much colder than they are today. Every winter, the canals, ponds and marshes would freeze over, and people who lived in the fenlands went about by skating. Some years, it was so cold that even the rivers froze. In those years, they would have frost fairs and ice markets, setting up stalls in the middle of lakes and even on the river Thames in London. Our story takes place in one of those years.

Three traders from the same village heard about an ice market taking place in a nearby town, and decided to make the journey. None of them had very much money for Christmas, and each one thought that by selling their wares, they might be able to afford a good dinner for their family. So they set out across the fens on their skates: a baker with her sack of bread, a grocer with his sack full of winter vegetables, and a butcher whose sack contained a large ham, ready to sell slice by slice at the market.

Sadly, as they skated up the river in the centre of the town where the market was, they met a crowd coming in the other direction. 'The ice market has been cancelled!' they shouted. 'The ice has cracked under the weight of the stalls, and the river is starting to run again! Quick - go the other way!'

In the confusion, the three friends were swept over to the side of the river.

'What a shame,' said the baker, 'now we won't be able to sell a thing. It'll be bread and water for us this year.'

'I had so hoped to give the children a good Christmas dinner,' said the grocer, 'but I suppose it will be vegetable stew as normal.'

'Hold on a minute,' said the butcher. 'Between us, we have all the ingredients for a feast. Why don't we bring our families together for dinner? We can meet at my house if you like.'

They all thought that was a great idea, and set off towards home again. However, in the crowds racing away from the cracking ice, the three friends were separated.

The baker skated along with her head down against the wind, but as she went, she heard a child crying. When she looked up, she saw a young mother dressed in rags, with nothing on her feet against the ice, trying to wrap a shawl around her little girl. The shawl was more holes than shawl.

'You poor things! Can I help you?' asked the baker.

'Bless you, madam, we have no home and no money. I sold my shoes this morning to feed my daughter, but they only fetched a few pennies,' said the mother.

'Here,' said the baker, 'take my bread,' and she took the loaves from her sack and handed them over.

'Are you sure? All of them?' cried the delighted mother.

'Yes! You can sell what you don't eat, and buy a warmer shawl,' said the baker. 'I only wish I could do more. But I can do this, and it won't matter, because my friends and I have agreed to have dinner together this year, and my bread was the least important part of the feast. We will still have plenty to eat.'

Meanwhile, the grocer was skating along the other side of the river, and he saw a family walking along the edge, carrying bundles. They looked very tired.

'Where are you going?' asked the grocer. 'It's quicker to skate than to walk!'

'We don't have any skates,' said the father of the family. 'We come from far away, from a much warmer country. We had to run away from soldiers, and we only have what we are carrying. We are going into the town to beg for somewhere to stay.'

'You poor things!' said the grocer. 'Here, take the vegetables from my sack and put them in your bundles. When you reach a safe place, they will make a warm stew to welcome you.'

'Are you sure? All of them?'

'Yes, I'm sure,' said the grocer, 'because I'm having dinner with my friends tonight, and there will be plenty to go around. We'll still have meat and bread.'

The butcher got caught up in the crowd, and turned down a frosty canal. He realised he'd gone the wrong way when he saw the dark, grimy buildings on each side of the canal. Children were working, pulling carts of coal and loading it onto barges.

'Children, why are you still working? It's Christmas!' called the butcher.

'We have to keep going, or our boss whips us,' said one of the boys. 'We haven't stopped since the spoonful of gruel we got for breakfast.'

'You poor things! Here, have this ham out of my sack,' said the butcher. 'You can cut slices from it very quickly, and eat as you go.'

'Wow! Are you sure?' said the boy.

'Absolutely,' said the butcher. 'I'm having dinner with my friends, and there will be plenty to go around. We still have bread and vegetables. We don't need meat to have a good meal.'

When the three friends arrived at the butcher's house and compared stories, they felt very silly.

'Now we have lost our dinner - even the things we would have given our own families!' cried the grocer, horrified.

'So you say, but friend, you're keeping something from us,' said the baker. 'Your sack is clearly still full. Did you hear what we'd done and decide to keep your goods for your own family?'

'Not at all! In fact, come to think of it, your sack looks suspiciously lumpy as well!' cried the offended grocer.

'Wait!' said the butcher, 'My sack is suddenly heavy too! It was empty a moment ago - what's going on?'

The baker opened her sack and pulled out bread - not just bread, but pastries, tarts, cakes and puddings!

The grocer opened his, and pulled out, not just winter vegetables, but greens and fruits as well!

And in the butcher's sack, they found, not just the ham, but a steaming cooked goose stuffed with onions, a long string of sausages and a huge pork pie.

'It's a miracle!' they shouted.

'Gather round, children,' said the baker as they spread the feast on their shared table, 'and look at what we've learned today. If we hadn't agreed to share with each other, we would never have given our own things away; and if we hadn't given our things away, we would not have been blessed with this miracle. Let's never stop sharing the good gifts we've been given.'

The message at the end of this story is obvious. It's a good one for a school assembly with a message of generosity, or for a church raising money for a local charity or foodbank at Christmas.

PRESENTS

Why do we give each other presents at Christmas? It's a good way of celebrating a special day. It reminds us that God gave us a gift at Christmas: the gift of his son Jesus to make peace between people and God forever.

There's another explanation I like, which is that it's Jesus' birthday, and Jesus said that whenever we do a kind thing for another person, it's as if we're doing it for him. So when we give each other Christmas presents, we're giving Jesus birthday presents! Mind you, when Jesus said that, he was talking about helping people who really need our help: the poor, the hungry, the lonely and the sick. That's why people often give money to charities at Christmas time too.

Finding just the right present can be tricky, as you'll see in the next story. What's the best present you've ever been given?

TEDDY SHOES

There was once a little girl called Josie, who loved her grandfather. She didn't get to see him very often, because he lived far away in the countryside, while the girl lived with her mother, father and three smaller sisters in the town.

These days, we would probably just get into a car and drive. But in those days, travel was more complicated. Grandfather took a horse and cart from his house to the train station. Then he got onto a steam train that chuffed through the fields all the way to the train station in the town. Finally, the girls' father would pick him up in their new motor car. They were especially proud of their motor car, because hardly anybody had one. It wasn't very reliable, and it drove very slowly indeed.

Because it took so long to travel, Grandfather only visited once a year, at Christmas time. And because he only visited once a year, he wasn't very good at remembering how old Josie and her sisters were. Because of that, his Christmas presents were rather strange. When Josie was three, he gave her a baby's rattle; when she was six and could already read and write, he brought her some bricks with the alphabet on them.

Josie's mother taught the girls to be very polite, and before Grandfather's visits, they would practise saying, 'Oh, *thank* you, Grandfather! It's *just* what I wanted!' so that they could sound as if they meant it, no matter what came out of the brightly wrapped boxes.

Last Christmas, Josie had only just managed to say her polite thank you. Grandfather had brought her a beautiful pair of shoes, just like the ones she had been craving in a shop window. They were shiny, with little buttons to do up the straps. Sadly, they were far, far too small for her feet; they were so small, they didn't even fit any of Josie's little sisters! Josie had tried to smile, but she felt like crying. She had kept the lovely shoes in a box under her bed, so that even if she couldn't wear them, she could look at them every now and then.

So, now that Christmas was coming again, Josie was excited for her grandfather's visit, but less excited for any presents he might bring!

Instead, she looked forward to sitting with him by the fireside and hearing his stories of the farm where he lived.

When the day finally came, Josie was allowed to ride in the slow, bumpy motor car to collect Grandfather from the station. She ran over to him on the platform, gave him a big hug and led him by the hand back to the car, where she snuggled under a rug with him and asked all about his journey. She didn't ask a thing about the big pile of boxes he had brought with him.

After the last morsel of Christmas pudding had been cleared away and the family was gathered by the Christmas Tree, Grandfather brought out a box and beckoned Josie over.

'Now, I know that for the last few years, you've been growing so fast that I can't keep up! The things I've brought for you haven't been right. So this time, I'm giving you something that will last, no matter how old you are or how big you grow. This is for you.' He handed the box to Josie, who hardly dared to lift the lid and have a look.

Inside the box was a beautiful, big teddy bear, with lifelike shiny eyes, a sweet turned-up nose and soft, silky fur.

'Oh, thank you, Grandfather!' said Josie - and she didn't have to pretend to mean it as she gave Grandfather, and her new bear, a big hug.

Grandfather was right. Josie loved her bear. No matter how old she was, no matter how big she grew, she kept her teddy and he was her best friend. One of the first things she did was to try the little shoes on him - they fitted him much better than they did her, so she let him wear them. She kept the bear until she was an old, old lady and he was an old, old bear. And you can still visit him today - he is in a museum in Ipswich with some other old bears. You'll know which one is the bear from this story, because he looks very loved, and he is still wearing a little pair of girls' shoes.

This story is a good one to tell with plenty of interaction, fun for nurseries or assemblies. Get the children to make noises for all the grandfather's travel: clip-clopping for the horse and cart, chuffing and whistling for the steam train and some loud engine noises for the motor car! With smaller groups, I have baby toys in shiny boxes for volunteers to open, and rehearse all the children in saying, 'Oh, thank you, Grandfather, it's just what I wanted!' no matter what gets pulled out. A real teddy bear is a bonus too.

The story is a good beginning for conversations about gratitude, or about what it's like to get a good present and how the giver has to know what you need, which can lead to discussing how God knows our every need, and how he knew the need of the world when he sent Jesus. Another good follow-up question to open discussion could be: 'Is there such a thing as a present that will last your whole life?'

IT'S NOT OVER YET!

TWELVE DAYS

Did you know that Christmas is not just one day? It's a whole season, just like Advent was! Christmas lasts for twelve days. It used to be celebrated for all twelve days, with feasting, parties and time off work. There are still some traditions left over from those days, which you can find if you look carefully. Think of the popular Christmas song about the partridge in the pear tree, for example. And can you remember which country I mentioned earlier, where Christmas dinner has twelve special foods?

These days, we often have to go back to work (and school) before the twelve days are over. But there are still ways to celebrate. We can leave the decorations up. We can carry on saying 'Happy Christmas'. We can go out with our friends, after Christmas Day was spent with family. And there are still some special occasions to look forward to.

NEW YEAR

People often have a party and stay up until midnight to listen to the clock chime twelve on New Year's Day. There are fireworks in many places, or the big London display to watch on television!

Just like Christmas traditions, New Year's traditions vary from place to place. In Spain, people try to eat twelve grapes before the clock has stopped chiming. In Denmark, they smash plates against (closed!) front doors at midnight; and in Brazil, people go to the beach and try to jump over seven waves, making a wish for each wave.

Here are some ideas you could try:

- Eat something round or ring-shaped, like a doughnut. In many countries, round foods symbolise the turning of the year, endings leading to new beginnings.
- Set yourself a challenge to do in the time it takes the clock to strike twelve (or, if you're not allowed to stay up until midnight yet, in twelve seconds!)
- Make a list of things you're grateful for in the year that has passed, and a list of your hopes for the year to come. Put them in a safe place (maybe packed away with the Christmas decorations) so that you can look at them again next year.
- Have a clean up: make some space to put your new presents away by donating some old toys, and start the year with a tidy space.
- Find out the time of the New Year in another country (some happen before ours, and some after, because of the time difference). Research a tradition from that country, or find out how to say 'Happy New Year' in that language and then celebrate it at the right moment.

EPIPHANY

In our nativity plays, the shepherds, angels and wise men come to the stable all together. But in the Bible, the wise men turned up quite a bit later, in a different part of the story and in a different book of the Bible! (Also, there might not have been three of them. All we know from the

Bible is that they brought three gifts. You can find the story in the Bible in chapter 2 of the Gospel of Matthew.)

Epiphany is not just one day, but a whole season, just like Advent and Christmas. Advent was all about the people who waited for Jesus, and Epiphany is all about the people who recognised him when he came. That's why it begins with the story of the wise men.

The visit of the wise men, also called kings or magi, is celebrated on January 6th, and in some countries, it's a bigger celebration than Christmas. Even in England, Epiphany has its own church service, its own music and its own stories, separate from Christmas.

In Spain and France, there is a 'king cake' with a bean, or a little figurine, hidden inside. Whoever gets the hidden object in their slice is then the king or queen of the party and wears a crown.

The wise men were not necessarily kings, though. They were people who studied the stars, so Epiphany celebrations can also involve going out at night to look at the starry sky. And they brought gifts of gold, frankincense and myrrh, so some people give gifts to represent them: money or jewellery for the gold, something to help with prayer or something that smells good for the frankincense, and something to use on the body (like soap or hand cream) for the myrrh.

There are plenty of stories that go with the celebration of Epiphany, too. Here are just two of them.

THE EPIPHANY STORY

Because there are so few details about the wise men in the Bible, but such a big festival for them, a tradition has grown up around their story, giving them names, backgrounds and add-on stories, a bit like fan fiction! When you have read this story, have a look at the real story in the Bible in Matthew chapter 2, and see if you can spot the differences.

On a starry night, on a winding road, three travellers met. All three were weary, having travelled many days. All three wore rich robes and carried telescopes, through which they anxiously examined the sky. All three carried treasure; and because all three were well-educated and wise, the moment they met, they argued.

Melchior, king of Persia, pointed at the star they had all been following. 'As soon as it rose in the sky, I knew what it meant!' he said. 'A new king has been born - a great and powerful king, far greater than any seen on earth before. That's why my gift for him is gold: treasure for a royal child.'

Gaspar, king of India, shook his head and muttered through his long, white beard. 'For years I have studied the wise writings of holy people. This star shows that a child has been born who will join earth to heaven forever. My gift, frankincense, lifts our prayers to heaven on sweet-smelling smoke, just as this child will link people to God so that every prayer is heard and God dwells with us on earth.'

Balthasar, who had travelled from one of his many palaces in Africa, looked sad. 'If only you were right, dear sirs. I can see from this star's alignment that this child is born to great suffering. His suffering will save many others, but I bring myrrh for the anointing of his wounds, for he will be hurt and will die - perhaps as he fights and wins a war.'

'Let us not argue, good sirs, for it seems that we are all following the same star, and that star will lead us to a child,' said Melchior, 'and that being the case, let us travel together.'

Gaspar agreed. 'The star nears Jerusalem, and there is a palace in that city. Since we all agree that this child will be special or important in some way, and has long been foretold, let us ask for him at the palace: their holy teachers will surely know about him there.'

'Very well,' said Balthasar, 'for kings and princes often go to war,' and the three travelled onwards along the same road.

When they reached the palace, they asked to see King Herod, and were brought into the magnificent throne room. They bowed, and explained that a star had led each of them to leave his own palace and travel to find a special child.

'We seek a new king, a mighty ruler,' said Melchior.

'We seek a holy child, God walking among us,' said Gaspar.

'We seek the one whose battle wounds will make him victorious,' said Balthasar. 'Do you know any child like that?'

Herod narrowed his eyes. 'I am a mighty ruler. My subjects worship me. I fight anyone who comes against me. Perhaps the star is mine.'

Melchior shook his head. 'It is a child that we seek, your majesty. His star has only just risen.'

'Well, there is no child here. But if you do find him, come back here and let me know, so that I can give him a gift of my own,' snarled King Herod, clenching his fists. The three wise kings backed away.

That night, the star came up and moved again. The wise kings followed it out of the city and over the hills to a little town called Bethlehem. There, it stopped above a small white house with a flat roof, on the edge of the town near a field of sheep. Melchior raised an eyebrow: 'Really? Here?'

'Let's knock on the door,' said Balthasar. 'We've been wrong once before. We should not ignore the star.'

The door was opened by a young woman with a toddler on her hip. Her eyes widened when she saw her visitors, with their fine clothes and treasures, but she seemed to be expecting them as well.

'Have you come to see Jesus?' she asked, resting her cheek on the little boy's head. 'Come in. You've found the right place. My name is Mary.' She called over her shoulder, 'Joseph, wake up! We have visitors!'

Melchior, Gaspar and Balthasar followed her inside the little house, full of wonder, and handed their gifts to the little boy.

'Here is gold, O mighty king,' said Melchior.

'Here is frankincense, O holy child,' said Gaspar.

Balthasar's eyes filled with tears as he placed the myrrh in front of Jesus, who put out a chubby hand and touched the king's wet cheek.

'Thank you,' whispered Balthasar.

'Why don't you stay the rest of the night here?' suggested Mary. 'It's nearly dawn, but we might all manage a little more sleep before the sun comes up.'

So they did, settling down on the rush-strewn floor together. They slept deeply, but first thing in the morning, all three kings sat bolt upright with a gasp at the same time.

'I had a dream!' said Melchior.

'Me too!' said Gaspar.

'And me!' said Balthasar.

'We must not go back to Jerusalem!' said Melchior.

'Absolutely not!' said Gaspar.

'King Herod wants to kill the child!' said Balthasar.

They stared at each other in wonder. They had all dreamed exactly the same dream.

'Could it be,' said Gaspar thoughtfully, 'that we were *all* right, all along?'

So the three wise kings travelled home by a different route, avoiding Jerusalem and the angry, jealous king Herod; and when the road separated three ways they parted as friends, and went back to their palaces to tell their own countries about the child who would be a mighty king, an everlasting God, and a wounded prince of peace.

As the introduction points out, this is not the Biblical Epiphany story, but the tradition that has grown up around it. We do not know the names of the magi, nor exactly what they were - kings, astrologers, scholars - nor even how many of them there were. Even the interpretation of the meaning of the gifts is not mentioned in Matthew's account, though it is widely accepted. However, Herod's reaction is just as Matthew tells it. I have left the slaughter that followed out of this book, but it is part of the Christmas story nonetheless. Herod should come across as very unpleasant in this telling.

This version of the story, and interpretation of the gifts, is a good way to start a discussion about the expectations of Jesus and what he came to do. You could ask children: which of the wise kings was right? Were they all right? What did Jesus do, or what happened to him, that was like what each of the kings said about him?

The very last sentence is a not-quite-accurate echo of Isaiah 9:6.

BABOUSHKA

Another tradition that has grown up around the wise men is telling stories about people (and animals) who met them on their travels, or travelled with them. Here is perhaps the best known of those stories, which comes from Russia.

Baboushka's house was always neat as a pin. The paint was always fresh, the windows were always gleaming, and the floors were always swept and mopped. If you went to visit, Baboushka would always open the door in her apron and headscarf, clutching a duster. It seemed that there was never a moment when she wasn't cleaning.

'It's because she has no children,' the younger women said. 'That's how she has so much time to keep things clean.'

The older women said, 'Poor Baboushka! She never had children to help her. That's why she has to spend all that time cleaning. She's doing the job of five people!'

None of them knew about Baboushka's secret cupboard. If they had known, they would have been amazed.

Early one morning, just as Baboushka was making her bed, there was a knock at her door. When she opened it, she was astonished to see three kings standing there, their crowns gleaming in the dawn light.

'May we spend the day resting at your house?' they asked. 'We have been following a star all night, and we need to sleep. Your house is the neatest on the street.'

Baboushka was flattered. 'Of course - come in! But what do you mean, "following a star"?'

The kings settled themselves in the spotless sitting room, their long robes brushing along the polished floorboards as they entered. They told their story to Baboushka.

'A new star has risen in the sky, and it's moving! We have studied the stars for many years, and we know that it means a special baby has been born. The star will show us where the child is, if we follow it until it stops. We have already travelled half the globe. We will surely find the baby soon.'

'A baby?' said Baboushka, her face brightening. 'I would love to send a gift to a special baby.'

'Come with us!' said one of the kings. 'We will leave as soon as the sun goes down and we can see the star again.'

Baboushka waited until the kings were sleeping, and then she went to her secret cupboard. She took a deep breath before she opened it.

Out tumbled an avalanche of baby things. Tiny clothes and bright toys, knitted boots and soft blankets, bottles and small spoons and a little silver porridge bowl. All the things she had bought and saved over the years, waiting for the baby she had never had.

But, oh dear, as well as all the toys and clothes, there was a cloud of dust. Baboushka had not opened her secret cupboard in years.

'None of these things is fit for a baby!' Baboushka said to herself. 'They all need to be cleaned before I can decide what to bring! And then I'll have to clean the floor again. Look at this mess I've made!'

When the kings woke up, they found Baboushka behind a pile of toys, dusting and polishing. Behind her, there was a tub of soapy water filled with little clothes and blankets. More were hanging out on a line in the garden.

'Baboushka, it's time to go!' said the kings. 'The star has risen in the sky!'

'Oh, just wait a bit longer, please,' said Baboushka, 'I still have all these to clean, and then I'll need to leave the house tidy. Can't we go tomorrow night?'

'The star will have moved on by then,' said the kings. 'We have to keep our eyes on it.'

But Baboushka wouldn't stop cleaning and sorting. The kings had to leave without her. It was only several days later, after all the little clothes were dry and she had packed the spotless things into a big basket and given the floor one last sweep, that she was ready to go.

Baboushka set out with her basket on her back, and looked up into the night sky. There was no special star. So she went down the street, knocking on her neighbours' doors and waking them up. 'Have you seen three kings? Which way did they go?'

At last, a little boy said that he'd seen the kings leaving, and pointed the way. Baboushka travelled on. Every time she came to a village or town, she asked after the kings and went the way she was told. She travelled for many weeks, the toys heavy on her back.

At long last, she entered a little town called Bethlehem, and she didn't have to wait long before finding somebody who knew what she was talking about.

'Oh yes, they were here. But that was weeks ago.'

'What about the baby they came to see?'

'The baby has gone. The visit of the kings made King Herod suspicious, and he wanted to kill the little boy, so his family ran away to a safe place. I don't know where they went.'

Baboushka felt close to tears. 'It's all my fault. I shouldn't have stayed and cleaned all those toys. I should have gone with the kings. Now I've missed my chance.'

'What will you do now?' asked the kind stranger.

She gathered herself together, wiped her eyes and picked up her basket. 'I have to keep going. I will search for the baby until I find him.' And she set off into the night.

They say that Baboushka still travels the world with her basket, asking sometimes for the kings, sometimes for the baby. Whenever she comes across a sleeping child, she takes a gift from her basket and leaves it there, just in case it is the child she's been looking for.

EPIPHANY BOXES

In our church, we started a tradition of Epiphany Boxes, which the children would make to give out to the adults. They also make a lovely gift to bring into old people's homes or to the church lunch club, etc, when they meet after Christmas.

We used origami star boxes (many instructions can be found by entering 'origami star box' into Google or Youtube; the four-pointed boxes are the simplest!). You have to begin with a large enough piece of paper for the box to contain the gifts you have selected, so a bit of experimentation is needed.

The contents of the box correlates with the three gifts of the kings and their symbolic meaning. We put in a gold (chocolate!) coin for the gold, a scented candle for the frankincense and a bar of soap, bottle of hand sanitiser or tube of hand cream for the myrrh.

The frankincense represents coming closer to God, so depending on numbers and costs, you could also offer a small wooden holding cross or a prayer card for that.

CANDLEMAS

Even though Christmas finishes after twelve days, the season of Epiphany (remember, it's about people who recognised Jesus) carries on until Candlemas. Candlemas is exactly 40 days after Christmas, so it falls on the 2nd of February. At Candlemas, we tell the last story we know from the Bible about Jesus when he was a baby, which happened 40 days after his birth. This is the story. You can find it in the Bible in Luke 2:22-38.

40 days after Jesus was born, Mary and Joseph took him to the temple in Jerusalem, to follow the custom with a special ceremony of presentation and purification.

In the temple were two very old people. One of them was Anna, a prophetess who had dedicated her whole life to serving God there. The other was Simeon. God had promised Simeon that he would not die until he had seen God's promises come true with his own eyes: so Simeon knew that he would see the Messiah, the one God had promised for so long.

When Mary and Joseph came into the temple carrying Jesus, Simeon looked up and saw them. At once, despite his great age, he got to his feet and hurried forwards, holding both his arms out in front of him. He couldn't take his eyes off Jesus. Mary placed the little bundle into Simeon's arms, and the old man gazed down at the baby.

'Now, God, I can go in peace. You have kept your promise!' Simeon murmured. 'I am looking at your salvation with my own eyes. This is the Light of the World.' With shining eyes, he looked up at Mary. 'This child will be so important to the whole of Israel, and the world. He will suffer, and so will you, so that God's promises can come true through him.'

At that moment, Anna hobbled over, waving her arms and shouting joyfully. 'Thank God! Thank God!' she called out, so that everyone in the temple would listen. 'This child is the one we've been waiting for! Our God has come to save us, at last! God has kept his promise!'